Kids Keeping Kids Safe

By K. L. Wheatley
Illustrations: Marianne Hallock
Cover Design: Bob Simeone

© 1998 Leading Edge
P.O. Box 70675
Eugene, OR 97401
(541) 461-9819
http://www.safetykidsclub.com

A Parent/Child Read-together Guide to Help Teach Children Personal Safety

Message to Parents

Kids Keeping Kids Safe is a comprehensive program designed to teach safety awareness to the entire family. Your children will enjoy learning personal safety procedures with this read-together parent/child guide!

Don't go too fast!

Examine the whole book to get an overview of all the ideas, then go through it slowly with your children. Every idea is important. Reinforce it several different ways. Discuss unfamiliar words. Play safety games. Color the pictures.

Children love stories, so make up your own similar to the ones in the book. Stories can be simple; your determination to keep your kids safe is more important than your literary skills. Ask the librarian for other materials to reinforce the same ideas. **Kids Keeping Kids Safe** was designed to open dialog between parent and child. Listen to your children and review their answers. Some activities may have multiple answers.

Personalize rules to fit your family.

The rules we suggest are recommended by safety experts, however, each family situation is unique. The **Safety Kids Club** and **Safety Sam** give your family the tools needed to work up your own **Family Safety Plan of Action**. It's every parent's responsibility to give specific warnings and precautions for their neighborhood and surrounding areas.

Have fun!

Make each session fun so your children will have happy memories of the time you spent with them learning safety rules. The more pleasant the associations they have with this book, the more often they will pick it up and review the ideas on their own—and the safer they will be!

Contents

Section 1

Help your children build self-esteem and develop a strong sense of family. Topics like <u>All about Me</u>, <u>My World</u>, and <u>How I Send a Letter</u> give them an understanding of who they are, who their parents are, where they live, and the special people in their lives.

Section 2

Safety Sam and the **Safety Kids Club** teach your children specific safety rules to follow with <u>Using the Phone</u>, <u>Opening the Door</u>, <u>Strangers</u>, <u>Checking First</u>, <u>The Buddy System</u>, <u>Going to and from School</u>, <u>Talking with Mom or Dad</u>, and <u>Kids Can Say "No!"</u> You'll want to personalize each topic by playing "What if" games, using examples of familiar people and places to help children fully understand each guideline.

Section 3

You and your children will feel safer after developing your **Family Safety Plan of Action,** with your family's specific safety rules.

Section 4

This comprehensive <u>Safety Test</u> is designed to determine your children's understanding of personal safety. How they answer these questions will show you what areas you need to work on.

Safety Sam's
Safety Kids Club
Top 10 Safety Tips

- 🐾 Safe Kids can always talk to their parents or another trusted grown-up about anything.

- 🐾 Safe Kids always "Check First."

- 🐾 Safe Kids know how to dial <u>9-1-1</u> in an emergency.

- 🐾 Safe Kids never talk to anyone they don't know well.

- 🐾 Safe Kids always use the "Buddy System."

- 🐾 Safe Kids say "No!" to anyone who tries to touch them in a way that makes them feel uncomfortable. Then they tell their parents or another trusted grown-up right away.

- 🐾 Safe Kids never open the door for anyone but a trusted friend or relative.

- 🐾 Safe Kids always tell their parents or another trusted grown-up if anyone asks them to keep a secret.

- 🐾 Safe Kids always follow their **Family Safety Plan of Action**.

- 🐾 Safe Kids know that their parents would never send anyone they don't know well to pick them up.

Section 1

-  All about Me

- My World

- How I Send a Letter

- My Fingerprints

All about Me

My first name is ———————————————————————

My last name is ———————————————————————

My middle name is ———————————————————————

My birth date is ———————————————————————

My mom's first name is ———————————————————————

My mom's last name is ———————————————————————

My dad's first name is ———————————————————————

My dad's last name is ———————————————————————

My address is ———————————————————————

My street is ———————————————————————

My city is ———————————————————————

My state is ———————————————————————

My zip code is ———————————————————————

My area code is ———————————————————————

My phone number is ———————————————————————

More about Me

My favorite color is ____

My favorite book is ____

My favorite food is ____

My best friend's name is ____

My favorite teacher is ____

My favorite animal is ____

My favorite sport is ____

My favorite place to go is ____

My special memory is ____

____

____

____

____

____

My World

This is me.

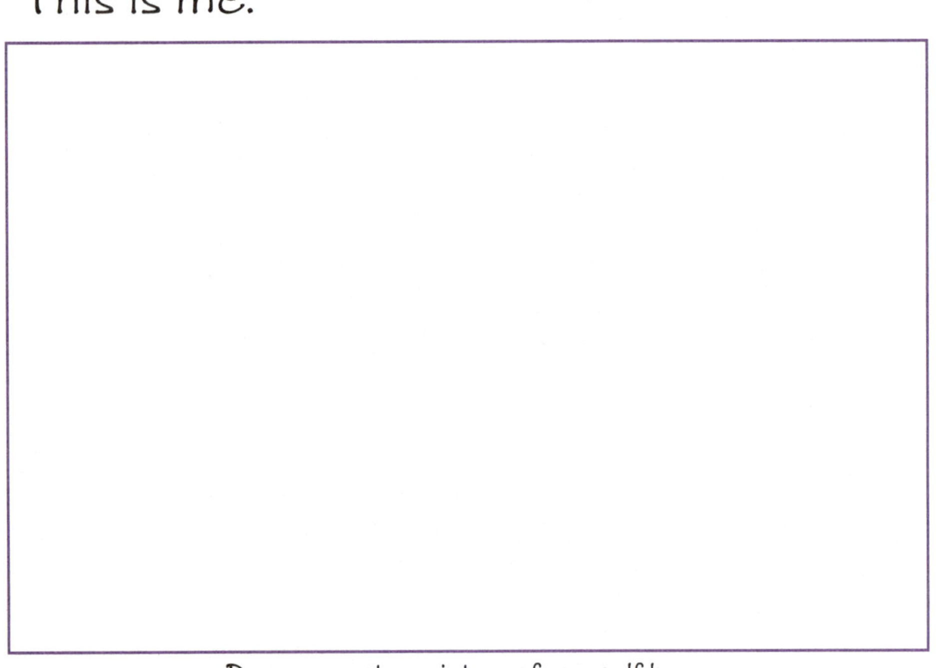

Draw or paste a picture of yourself here.

This is my family.

Draw or paste a picture of your family here.

Page 8

This is my house.

Draw or paste a picture of your house here.

This is my school.

Draw or paste a picture of your school here.

How I Send a Letter

My home address is ___________________________ .

My street I live on is ___________________________ .

___________________________ street is in the

city of ___________________________ .

My city is in the state of ___________________________ .

My zip code is ___________________________ .

This is how I would address an envelope to my mom or dad.

Place stamp here.

This is a list of special people I know.

Name   Relationship

______________________   ______________________

______________________   ______________________

______________________   ______________________

______________________   ______________________

This is how I would address an envelope to a special person.

____

____

____

Place stamp here.

____

____

____

My Fingerprints

No two zebras look exactly alike. Their stripes are different.

My Fingers Have Stripes Too

The stripes on people's fingers are too small to see without a magnifying glass, but they are there. When I touch something, I leave fingerprints on it.

No one in the whole world has fingerprints exactly like mine! I have____________ different fingerprints, one on each finger.

Safety Sam Says...

I think you are great!
You are very special. There's no
one in the world just like you.

Circle "Yes" or "No"

Does anyone else have eyes the same color
as yours?   Yes   No

Does anyone else have fingerprints just like
yours?   Yes   No

Does anyone else have the same phone
number you do?   Yes   No

Does anyone else look just like you?   Yes   No

Does anyone else have the same address
you do?   Yes   No

Does anyone draw pictures just like yours?   Yes   No

Is anyone else in the world just like you?   Yes   No

Section 2

Using the Phone

Safety Rule #3:

Safe Kids know that in an emergency they can dial
9-1-1 or "O" – WITHOUT using any money.

Using a Pay Phone

Morgan and Kenneth were walking to the park when they saw a little boy crying at a pay phone. He looked lost and scared.

"What's the matter?" asked Kenneth.

"I'm trying to call home. This phone isn't working."

Morgan said, "You need money to use this phone."

"But you don't need money to dial '<u>O</u>' to call the operator," said Kenneth, "and you don't need money to dial <u>9-1-1</u> in an emergency."

Morgan and Kenneth remembered their safety rules and helped the little boy call home.

Safety Kids Club Safety Rules:

- Usually you need money to use a pay phone.

- You can dial <u>9-1-1</u> in an emergency without using any money.

- You can dial "<u>O</u>" to speak with an operator in an emergency without using any money.

- You can dial "<u>O</u>", and an operator will help you call your family "collect" without using any money.

More about Using the Phone

My phone number is ____________________________________.

My area code is ____________________________________.

In an emergency, I dial ______________________________.

<u>9-1-1</u> costs ________________________ at a pay phone.

To make a collect call, I dial ________________________.

Dialing "<u>O</u>" costs ______________________ at a pay phone.

When I need help, I can call someone I trust.

Name	Phone number
________________________	________________________
________________________	________________________
________________________	________________________

Safety Sam Says...

Good job learning phone safety!
Isn't it nice to know we can always
use the telephone to get help?

Draw a line to numbers you would call if ...

You miss the bus.

You're at the park, and your
friend falls and breaks an arm.

You are at your friend's house,
and his neighbor said he will pay
you to rake leaves for him.

You are home alone and scared
of a person you can see outside.

You are lost at the mall and don't
have money for a pay phone.

Home
Phone number

Mom or
dad at work
Phone number

9-1-1

Special
person
Phone number

Operator
Number

(There may be more than one answer each time.)

You've learned to use the
phone to call for help!

Answering the Phone

Safety Rule #14:

Safe Kids know that they don't need to tell a caller
their parents are not home.

Answering the Phone

Alexandra was home alone after school when her mom went to run some errands.

The phone rang, and Alexandra answered, "Hello?"

The caller said, "Hi, is your mom home?"

Alexandra remembered her safety rules and said, "My mom can't come to the phone right now. Please call back later."

Safety Kids Club
Safety Rules:

- Safe Kids never let a caller know they are home alone.

- Safe Kids always hang up if they hear scary or funny noises on the phone.

- If an unfamiliar caller is asking questions, Safe Kids say, "My parents can't come to the phone right now. Please call back later."

I Know My Phone Safety

- If I'm home alone and answer the phone, I always tell the caller, "My mom (or dad) can't come to the phone right now. Call back later." I never let a caller know I'm alone.

- I always know where emergency phone numbers are posted.

- If I hear a funny noise on the phone, I hang up.

- If I hear scary talk, or just don't like how I feel about the call, I hang up.

- If someone calls and says nothing on the phone, I hang up.

- I know how to call my mom (or dad) at work.

- I know how to make a long distance phone call.

- I know how to make a collect call.

- I know how to use a pay phone.

- I know how and when to call 9-1-1.

Safety Sam Says...

Good work! You know you don't have to let a caller know your mom or dad isn't home. You just use your family <u>Phone Script</u>.

Uh, oh. Willie dropped his family phone script and the words got all mixed up! Can you help him put them back together in the right order?

the · phone · back · right · come · can't · Mom · to · Please · call · later. · now.

Write the words in the boxes below:

Congratulations! You've learned to answer the phone safely!

Strangers at the Door

Safety Rule #7

Safe Kids know that when you are home alone, never open the door for <u>anyone</u>, except a trusted friend or relative.

Opening the Door

Sixteen-year-old Colin was home baby-sitting his little brother, Nicholas, when the door bell rang. Colin wasn't expecting anyone. Nicholas ran to the door to see who was there.

"Wait," Colin said. "Remember our safety rules! Never open the door until you know it is a trusted friend or relative."

Safety Kids Club Safety Rules:

- Safe Kids always keep doors locked when home alone.

- Safe Kids never open the door unless the person is a trusted friend or relative.

- If there is someone at the door who won't go away, Safe Kids call a parent or a trusted neighbor.

- If Safe Kids feel scared or threatened, they dial 9-1-1.

- Safe Kids never let strangers into the house to use the phone or bathroom, or for any reason.

- Safe Kids never open the door for anyone unless their parents have given them permission.

Who Can Come In?

If someone knocks at the door when I am at home alone, I will check to see who is there before I open it. These are the only people who can come in:

____

____

____

____

____

Congratulations! You've learned not to open the door for people you don't know well!

People We Don't Know Well

Safety Rule #4

Safe Kids never talk to strangers or anyone they don't know well.

People We Don't Know Well

Toni, Amanda, and Taylor were walking home from school when a car came by and stopped. The driver was someone they didn't know. He was a stranger!

"Can you tell me how to get to the library?" the stranger asked.

The girls, remembering their safety rules, ran away from the stranger and told their parents.

Safety Kids Club Safety Rules:

- Safe Kids know grown-ups should ask <u>only</u> other grown-ups for help.

- Safe Kids never talk to someone they don't know well.

- If approached by a stranger, Safe Kids <u>always take a few steps back</u>. They get ready to run away.

- If Safe Kids feel threatened, they run to a safe place and get help.

- Safe Kids know that sometimes strangers who look friendly try to trick kids.

- Safe Kids know that their mom or dad would never send someone they don't know well to get them.

- Safe Kids <u>never</u> accept candy or anything else from someone they don't know well.

I Promise to Stay Safe Around People I Don't Know Well

Unless my mom or dad (or another grown-up I trust) is with me, I will stay away from grown-ups and older kids I don't know well.

- I won't go near their car—and I will never get into their car.
  (My mom or dad would never send someone I don't know well to pick me up!)

- I won't help them look for a lost pet or give directions.
  (Grown-ups should ask other grown-ups for help.)

- I won't let them take my picture.

- I won't take money, candy, or gifts from them.
  (They might pretend to be my friends to get me to go with them.)

- I won't do jobs for them, or go into their house or yard for any other reason.
  (They might promise to pay a lot of money just to trick me.)

- I won't let them follow me.
  (I will run away and tell a grown-up I trust as soon as I can!)

- I will tell a grown-up I trust if I see them hanging around the school yard or playground.

Safe People

Strangers who come to me when my dad and mom aren't there may try to trick me, so I won't talk to them. But if I need help, I might <u>have</u> to talk to someone I don't know well. Here are safe people to ask for help.

- A person with children.

- A policeman or security guard in a uniform.

- A sales clerk behind a counter of a store, or a receptionist behind a desk.

On a city bus, I will try to do this:

- Not sit by myself. A scary person might come and sit by me at the next stop.

- Sit near the driver.

- Sit near a person with children.

- Sit near someone who looks like a grandmother.

Safety Sam Says...

Good job! You know you should stay with trusted friends and family members. Here's a puzzle to help you practice.

Is each person a family member, a trusted friend, or a person you don't know well? Draw a line to the right answer.

A man who says he is a policeman but doesn't have a police car or uniform

Grandma

Dad

Ice cream man

Mailman

Newspaper delivery person

Aunt_______________

Principal

Neighbor in _______________ house

Clerk at _______________ store

Teacher

Person I don't know who has lost a kitty and wants me to help find it

You have learned not to help people you don't know well!

Checking First

Safety Rule #2

Safe Kids know to always "check first."

Always "Check First"

Lindsay lived next door to Kelli. One day Lindsay and her mother were going grocery shopping. Lindsay asked Kelli if she would like to come along.

Kelli was very excited and got into the car without checking first.

While Kelli was gone, her mother was very worried. Kelli had forgotten one of the most important safety rules. Always "check first!"

Safety Kids Club Safety Rules:

- Safe Kids never go anywhere without checking first.

- Safe Kids always "check first" before going to a friend's house to play.

- Safe Kids never go into anyone's house without checking first.

- Safe Kids never get into anyone's car without checking first.

I Always "Check First"

- I need to ________________ before I go anywhere.

- Before I go into anyone's house, I need to ________________.

- Before I get into anyone's car, I need to ________________.

- Before accepting candy, money, or gifts from anyone, I need to ________________.

- If my ball goes into a neighbor's yard, before I go get it, I need to ________________ with ________________.

- Before I stop anywhere on my way home, I need to ________________.

Safety Sam Says...

Good job! Checking first before going anywhere will help keep you safe! Here's a puzzle to help you remember.

Directions: Fill in the blanks in the sentences below with words from the word box.

Word Box

friend	anywhere
tells	check
asks	always

When Bobby wants to go to the park, he _ _ _ _ mom.
9 5

Tammie _ _ _ _ _ _ her dad before she goes _ _ _ _ _ _ _ _ _.
13 2   1   7   12 8

Sara and Lizzie always _ _ _ _ _ with Grandma before they go.
6

Tim _ _ _ _ _ _ _ lets his mom know when he's going with a _ _ _ _ _ _
3   4   10   11
to the playground.

Now, use the numbered letters and write the mystery words here!

_ _ _ _ _ _   _ _ _ _ _   _ _ _ _ _
1 2 3 1 4 5   6 7 8 6 9   10 11 12 5 13

You've learned to "check first" before going somewhere!

The Buddy System

Safety Rule #5

Safe Kids always use the Buddy System.

Using the Buddy System

Jessica went with her cousins, Maria and Lupe, to a movie on Saturday afternoon.

Maria got up to use the restroom. Jessica said, "Wait, Maria. Did you forget about the Buddy System?"

"Gosh, I forgot the safety rule!" said Maria. "Safe Kids never go anywhere without a buddy."

Safety Kids Club Safety Rules:

- Safe Kids know they are always safer with a buddy when walking home, playing or out in public.

- Safe Kids always use the Buddy System when walking to and from school.

- Safe Kids never go to a public restroom alone. They always take a buddy.

- Safe Kids never play at the park or playground without a buddy.

Safety Sam Says...

Good job! You know that staying with a Buddy is smart—and fun!

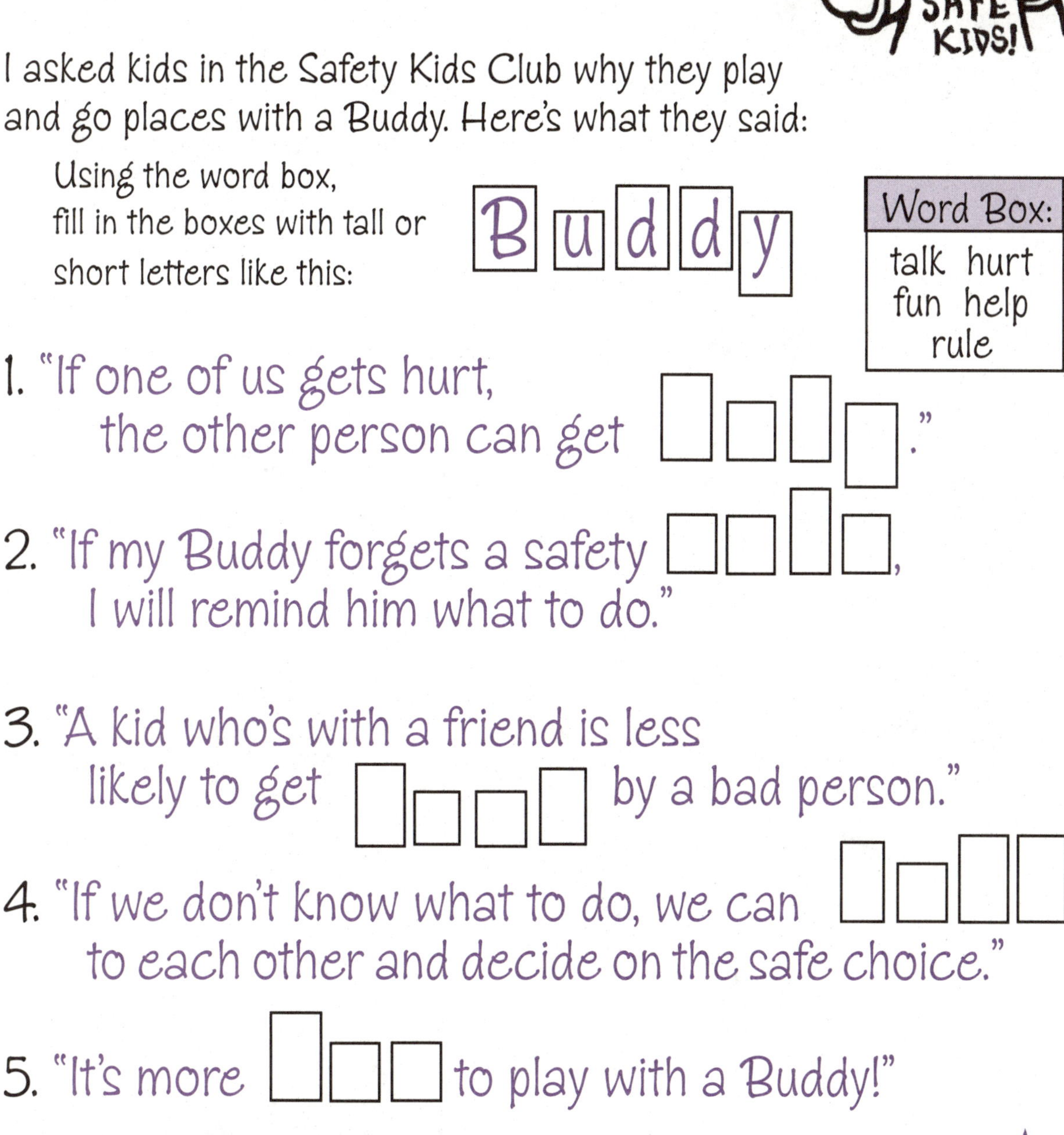

I asked kids in the Safety Kids Club why they play and go places with a Buddy. Here's what they said:

Using the word box, fill in the boxes with tall or short letters like this: Buddy

Word Box:
talk hurt
fun help
rule

1. "If one of us gets hurt, the other person can get ☐☐☐."

2. "If my Buddy forgets a safety ☐☐☐☐, I will remind him what to do."

3. "A kid who's with a friend is less likely to get ☐☐☐☐ by a bad person."

4. "If we don't know what to do, we can ☐☐☐☐ to each other and decide on the safe choice."

5. "It's more ☐☐☐ to play with a Buddy!"

Congratulations! You've learned to always stay with a Buddy!

To and from School

Safety Rule #12

Safe Kids always go straight home from school.

Never Take Shortcuts

Shane and Bobby walk to school together every day. They always take the same route and never take shortcuts. They walk facing traffic and cross at the same place every day.

One day they saw Rhys, a classmate, walking through a vacant lot.

"Rhys!" Shane called. "Come and walk with us!"

"Come on, Rhys," said Bobby. "It's not safe to walk alone or take shortcuts."

The three boys walked to school together. They talked about other safety rules for walking to and from school.

Safety Kids Club Safety Rules:

- Safe Kids always go straight home from school.

- Safe Kids know it is much safer to walk with a buddy.

- Safe Kids never take shortcuts.

- Safe Kids always take the same route.

- Safe Kids always follow their **Family Safety Plan of Action.**

My to and from School Safety Rules

- 🐾 I always go straight home from school unless I have checked first with my mom or dad.

- 🐾 I never take shortcuts through fields, alleys, or empty lots.

- 🐾 I know it is much safer to take the same route every day.

- 🐾 I never walk alone. I always use the Buddy System.

- 🐾 If I am approached by a man or a woman I do not know, I always keep my distance.

- 🐾 If I feel threatened, I run home or go to a safe place and get help right away.

- 🐾 If someone I don't know wants to pick me up because of an "emergency," I will go to the office and tell a secretary, a teacher, or a trusted adult right away.

- 🐾 If I miss my bus, I will go to the office and call home. If no one is home, I will call_______________.

Safety Sam Says...

Good job! You have learned to go to and from school safely.

Which route do Scott and Craig take going to school? Draw it with a pencil. Show which side of the street they should walk on and where they should cross the street.

How should they walk home after school? What might go wrong if they don't follow the safe path?

Congratulations!

You've learned to go to and from school safely!

Safety on the Internet

Safety Rule # 11
Safe Kids follow
on-line Safety Rules.

Safety on the Internet

Brent often talked to his new friend Jose on the Internet. They both liked computer games. One day Brent read this E-mail from Jose:

"Can you come to my house and try my new game?"

Brent was sure he would like Jose, but he had never met him in person, so he knew that it was not safe to go to his house. Brent sent back this E-mail:

"My dad and I will meet you at the library instead."

Safety Kids Club Safety Rules:

- Safe Kids don't give personal information to strangers on the Internet.

- Safe Kids never give their address or phone number on-line.

- Safe Kids never send a picture of themselves over the Internet or tell people they don't know what they look like.

- Safe Kids never arrange a meeting with anyone they have talked with on the internet.

- Safe Kids tell parents or other trusted grown-ups about any bad messages they receive.

Safety Sam Says...

Good job! You have to be smart to use computers so well.
You need to be smart about your on-line safety too!

When you get E-mail from a computer friend you have never met, can you tell whether your friend is...

A boy or a girl?   Yes   No

A young kid or an old person?   Yes   No

A nice or bad person?   Yes   No

Should you ever go to an Internet friend's house if your parents have never met the friend?   Yes   No

(The answer to all these questions is the same!)

Congratulations! You've learned to stay safe on the internet!

Talking with Mom or Dad

Safety Rule # 1

Safe Kids know they can always talk to their parents or another trusted grown-up about anything.

Talking with Mom or Dad

Billy went next door to see if his friend Chris wanted to play. He noticed that Chris looked unhappy. "What's wrong?" asked Billy.

"Uncle Jerry told me a secret and told me not to tell anyone, and it is bothering me."

Billy said, "This must be a secret too big to handle! You need to tell your parents!"

"But he told me not to tell!" said Chris.

"Your mom and dad are here to help you," said Billy. "Remember, you can always talk to them or another trusted adult about anything that is bothering you. One of the most important safety rules is <u>never keep secrets from your parents!</u>"

Safety Kids Club
Safety Rules:

- Safe Kids <u>never</u> keep secrets from their parents.

- Safe Kids know parents are here to help kids.

- If Safe Kids have a problem that seems too big to handle on their own, they know they can always talk to their parents or another trusted grown-up.

I Know I Can Talk to Mom or Dad

- 🐾 I know I can always talk to my parents or a trusted grown-up about anything.

- 🐾 I know I am very special.

- 🐾 I know my parents love me very much.

- 🐾 I know my parents will always listen to what I say.

- 🐾 I know I never have to feel alone.

- 🐾 I know that my parents are here to help me, and they will do everything they can to keep me safe and happy.

Safety Sam Says...

Some things aren't scary. They are funny, or strange, or just interesting. Mom and Dad like to hear about ordinary things–but they must ALWAYS be told about scary things! If these things happen, should you tell your parents? Circle your answer.

Yes   Maybe   A girl wore a funny hat to class and the teacher made her take it off.

Yes   Maybe   A man at the park tried to make my friend and me go into the restroom with him, but we ran away.

Yes   Maybe   A stranger has been hanging around the school for two days talking to kids.

Yes   Maybe   Our teacher was sick so we had a substitute teacher. She looked kind of like Grandma.

Yes   Maybe   Our neighbor has been saying weird things that make me feel uncomfortable. But he says I can't tell anyone what we talk about!

Congratulations!

You've learned to tell a trusted grown-up about scary things!

Kids Can Say "No!"

Safety Rule #6

Safe Kids know that if anyone makes them feel uncomfortable, they should say "No!" and run and tell a trusted grown-up.

Kids Can Say "No!"

Jill saw her friend Yolanda at the playground sitting on a bench crying. Jill walked over to see if she could help. "What's wrong?" asked Jill.

"My baby-sitter always hugs and kisses me, but it doesn't feel nice like when Mom and Dad do it. It makes me feel uncomfortable."

Jill said, "You don't have to let anybody touch you in a way that seems wrong. Kids can say 'No!' You need to tell your mom or dad about that baby-sitter!"

Safety Kids Club
Safety Rules:

- Safe Kids know they do not have to hug or kiss anyone if they do not want to.

- Safe Kids say "NO!" if anyone tries to touch them in a way that makes them feel uncomfortable.

- Safe Kids always tell their parents right away if anyone makes them feel uncomfortable.

I Know I Can Say "No!"

- I always tell my mom, dad, or a trusted grown-up if anyone makes me feel uncomfortable.

- I know I don't have to hug or kiss anyone if I feel uncomfortable.

- I know if I have a problem too big to handle by myself, I can always tell my parents or a trusted grown-up.

- I know the difference between a good touch and a bad touch.

- If an adult or older child does something to me that makes me feel uncomfortable, I will tell a trusted adult right away.

- I know that what my bathing suit covers is private. No one has the right to touch my private parts.

- If someone tries to touch my private parts, I will say "No!" and tell a trusted grown-up right away.

I Don't Have to Keep "Bad Secrets"

I know I must tell a "bad secret" right away, even if someone says they will hurt me or my family if I tell.

I can tell my parents or another trusted adult without getting in trouble. It isn't my fault if someone else does something bad.

I know I am a very special person.

I have my own rights and feelings.

I trust my feelings.

More Ways to Say "No!"

If a grown-up or big kid wants you to do something that isn't right, here are some other ways to say "No."

All Kids Have Rights

- All kids have the right to feel safe.

- All kids have the right to talk to their parents or another trusted grown-up about anything.

- All kids have the right to be heard.

- All kids have the right to say NO.

- All kids have the right to BE SAFE.

Safety Sam Says...

Many grown-ups love you. You are very special to them! These are the people to talk to if you are hurt or frightened. Don't keep a secret from trusted grown-ups!

Trusted grown-ups are people you have known for a long time. They have never hurt you or asked you to keep a bad secret. They have shown you that they love you, and you can trust them.

Some kids have <u>one</u> special grown-up. Some have many. Who are the trusted grown-ups in your life?

<u>Family and close relatives:</u>

Mom_______________________

Dad _______________________

Grandpa____________________

Grandma____________________

Uncle______________________

Aunt_______________________

Brother____________________

Sister______________________

<u>People at school:</u>

Teacher ____________________

Counselor__________________

Principal___________________

<u>Special friends:</u>

____

____

____

Note to Parents: You should help your child recognize a <u>few</u> special grown-ups who can be confided in. Circle the most appropriate people on this list. Write in <u>specific names</u> of relatives, teachers, etc.

Congratulations

You know you can talk to trusted grown-ups about important things!

Section 3

Our Family Safety Plan of Action

The ___________ Family Safety Plan of Action

- Our Family's Safety Rules

- Our Family's Important Phone Numbers

- Our Family's Phone Script

- Our Family's Rules to Follow When Home with a Baby-sitter

- Our Family's Safety Rules for Going to and from School

- Our Family's Safety Rules to Follow When Home Alone

- Our Family's Rules for Using the Internet

Our Family's Safety Rules

1. ____

2. ____

3. ____

4. ____

5. ____

6. ____

7. ____

8. ____

9. ____

10. ____

Our Family's Important Phone Numbers

Mom's work #_________________   Mom's other #_________________

Dad's work #_________________   Dad's other #_________________

Other #_________________   Other #_________________

Relative's #_________________   Relative's #_________________

Neighbor's #_________________   Neighbor's #_________________

In an Emergency, Dial 9-1-1

Other Important Phone Numbers

Police Dept._____________   #_________________

Fire Dept._____________   #_________________

Doctor_____________   #_________________

To phone for help if we need it (even if we don't have money)!

____
(Sign your names here)

Our Family's Phone Script

This is what I tell callers when my mom and dad are not home:

____

____

____

____

Safety Sam's Phone Script

"My mom and dad can't come to the phone right now. Can I take a message?"

To answer the phone safely if we're alone and someone we don't know well calls!

____

(Sign your names here)

Our Family's Safety Rules to Follow When Home with a Baby-sitter

1. _______________________________________

2. _______________________________________

3. _______________________________________

4. _______________________________________

5. _______________________________________

6. _______________________________________

7. _______________________________________

We Promise... To follow our family's safety rules when we are with a baby-sitter.

____

(Sign your names here)

Our Family's Safety Rules for Going to and from School

1. _______________________________________

2. _______________________________________

3. _______________________________________

4. _______________________________________

I usually leave for school at _________________ o'clock.

Three SAFE PLACES on my way to school:

1. _______________________________________

2. _______________________________________

3. _______________________________________

____

More Rules for Going to and from School

Three SAFE PEOPLE on my way to school:

1. ____

2. ____

3. ____

Three SAFE PLACES to use a phone:

1. ____

2. ____

3. ____

Three SAFE PLACES to cross the street:

1. ____

2. ____

3. ____

More Rules for Going to and from School

Places where I should be extra careful:

1. ____

2. ____

3. ____

I need to stay far away from these isolated places:

1. ____

2. ____

When I arrive home, I need to check-in with:

1. ____

2. ____

Other rules to follow:

1. ____

2. ____

We Promise... To go to and from school safely, using the route we decided on.

____

(Sign your names here)

Our Family's Safety Rules to Follow When Home Alone

1. ____

2. ____

3. ____

4. ____

5. ____

6. ____

Our family's emergency
numbers are always posted

____
(where?)

More Rules to Follow When Home Alone

If I come home, and no one is there, I will:

1. ____

2. ____

3. ____

When I'm alone, before I go anywhere, I will:

1. ____

2. ____

3. ____

I will always leave a note on the _______________________
before going anywhere.

I will always check-in with _______________________
by _______________ o'clock.

We Promise... Not to let people we don't know well come in the house if we're alone.

____

Our Family's Rules for Using the Internet

When I can use the computer:

1. ____

2. ____

3. ____

Types of web sites I can visit:

1. ____

2. ____

3. ____

Types of web sites I cannot visit:

1. ____

2. ____

3. ____

More Rules for Using the Internet

Information I must never give to people that I have talked to on the Internet:

1. ____

2. ____

3. ____

4. ____

Precautions I must take before meeting an Internet friend in person:

1. ____

2. ____

Other Internet safety rules:

1. ____

2. ____

To follow safety rules when using the Internet.

____

                    (Sign your names here)

Section 4

Safety Kids Club
Safety Test

This comprehensive <u>Safety Test</u> is designed to determine your children's understanding of personal safety. How each child answers these questions will show you the areas that you need to work on with your children to keep them safe.

Safety Kids Club
Safety Test
Phone Safety

1. If I am home alone, and someone calls and wants to talk to my parents, I will ________________________________

____

____

________________________________ .

2. If I am home alone and hurt myself or need help, I will __________

____

____

________________________________ .

3. If I am away from home and don't have any money to call home, I will ________________________________

____

________________________________ .

Strangers at the Door

1. If I am home alone, and I hear a knock on the door, I will __________ __________ __________ __________ __________.

2. If I am home alone, and a delivery person knocks on the door, I will __________ __________ __________.

3. If I am home alone, and a man or woman I do not know knocks on the door, I will __________ __________ __________.

Safety Kids Club
Safety Test
Say "No" to Strangers

1. If I am playing, and a person I don't know well is watching me, I will____

    ____

    ____ .

2. If a person I don't know well asks me for directions, I will ________

    ____

    ____

    ____ .

3. If I am in a store, and a person I don't know well in a wheelchair offers me money to help carry groceries to the car, I will ________

    ____

    ____ .

4. If a person I don't know well comes to my school to pick me up and says my mom sent them, I will_______________________________

    ____

    ____

    ____ .

Say "No" to Strangers

5. If a person I don't know well asks me to help find a lost puppy, I
   will ____

   ____ .

6. If a person I don't know well offers me candy or a toy I really
   want, I will ____

   ____ .

7. If I need help, but no one I know is there, I will ask one of these
   people to help: ____

   ____

   ____ .

8. If a stranger says to come with him because he is a policeman,
   but he doesn't have a uniform or police car, I will _______________

   ____

   ____ .

Safety Kids Club
Safety Test
"Check First"

1. If my teacher asks me to stay after school, I will __________

____

______________________________________ .

2. If my friend wants me to go to his or her house after school, I will ______________________________________

____

______________________________________ .

3. If I want to ride my bike with my friend after school, I will __________

______________________________________ .

______________________________________ .

4. If my neighbor offers me money to do yard work, I will __________

____

______________________________________ .

Safety Kids Club
Safety Test
Buddy System

1. If I'm walking home from school, I will__________________________

____.

2. If I'm going to a friend's house, I will _______________________

____.

3. If I'm going to the park or playground, I will__________________

____.

4. If I'm in a public place and need to use the restroom, I will ______

____.

Safety Kids Club
Safety Test

To and from School

1. After school, I will go _______________________________
_______________________________.

2. If I'm walking home from school, and some classmates ask me
to take a shortcut, I will _______________________________
_______________________________.

3. If I'm walking home from school, and my friend wants me to stop
at his or her house, I will _______________________________
_______________________________.

4. If someone I don't know comes to pick me up at school and says
my parents sent them, I will _______________________________
_______________________________.

5. If someone I don't know tries to get me into his or her car, I will
____
_______________________________.

Safety Kids Club
Safety Test
Internet Safety

1. If someone I meet on the Internet wants me to send a picture of
   myself, I will ____

   ____ .

2. If someone I meet on the Internet wants me to give my phone
   number and address, I will ______________________________________

   ____ .

3. If an on-line friend wants to meet me in person, I will ____________

   ____

   ____ .

4. If someone sends me scary or bad things by E-mail, I will__________

   ____

   ____ .

Safety Kids Club
Safety Test
Talking with Mom or Dad

1. If something is bothering me, and I feel it is embarrassing, I will

____

____ .

2. If someone tells me to keep a secret from my parents, I will

____

____ .

3. If someone makes me feel uncomfortable, I will _______________

____

____ .

Kids Have Rights

1. If someone wants to hug or kiss me, and I do not want them to,

   I will____

   ____ .

2. If I have a bad feeling about someone, I will ___________________

   ____ .

3. If someone tries to touch my private parts, I will _______________

   ____

   ____ .

4. If someone tells me to keep a secret, I will ____________________

   ____ .

Safety Sam's Glossary of Important Words and Terms

Can you tell your mom or dad what these words or terms mean?

9-1-1	Run and Tell
Buddy System	Safe Kids
Check First	Safe Place
Collect Call	Safe People
Emergency	Say No
Family Safety Rules	Secret
Isolated Place	Shortcut
Kids Rights	Someone I Don't Know Well
Long Distance Call	Stranger
On-line Safety	Surprise
Operator	Trusted Adult
Phone Script	Uncomfortable